KV-557-948

Abernethy Primary School

Nethy Bridge
www.abernethy.highland.sch.uk

ABERNETHY PRIMARY SCHOOL
NETHY BRIDGE
INVERNESS-SHIRE
PH25 3ED

PLANET
EARTH

STEVE PARKER

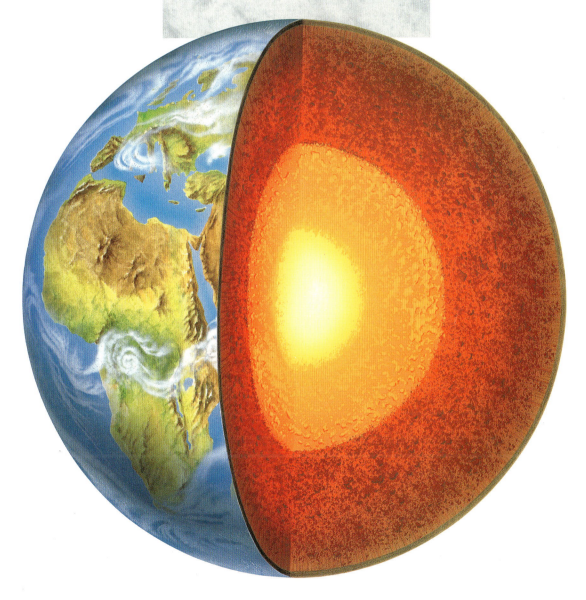

Heinemann

ACKNOWLEDGEMENTS

The publisher would like to thank the following individuals and organizations
for providing the photographs used in this book:
Heather Angel: 47 top right. Ardea / Bob Gibbons: 19 top right.
Bridgeman Art Library: 4 top right. John Cleare: 35 top right.
Bruce Coleman Ltd / Bob and Clara Calhoun: 39 centre left, / Geoff Dore: 28 below left, /
Harald Lange: 15 top right, / Andy Price: 15 top left, / Hans Reinhard: 43 top right.
Ecoscene / Jones: 46 top right, / Sally Morgan: 19 below right, / Nick Hawkes: 29 below right, /
Hulme: 45 top right, / Alan Towse: 45 below right.
Mary Evans: 4 below left. Frank Lane Picture Agency / Panda/C Cocchia: 44 top right.
Geoscience Features: 12 top left, 12 top centre, 12 top right, 21 centre right, 21 top right, 22 top right.
Natural Science Photos / Paul Kay: 21 below right.
NHPA / N A Callow: 15 below right, / Brian Hawkes: 28 top right / Otto Rogge: 18 top right.
Planet Earth Pictures / Pieter Folkens: 7 below right.
Science Photo Library / Jim Amos: 22 below right, / Martin Bond: 39 centre right, / Ray Ellis: 39 below centre, /
Dr Fred Espenak: 5 below right, / Simon Fraser: 6 centre, 9 below right, 20, 30 top centre, 43 centre left, /
David Hardy: 11 below right, / Keith Kent: 36 below right, / Peter Menzel: 10 top right, 13 top right, /
Dr Morley: 31 below right, / Nasa: 43 below left.
Scotland in Focus: 13 below right. Viewfinder Colour Photo Library: 21 centre left.

ILLUSTRATORS:

Julian Baker: 16-17, 24-25, 32-33, 40-41.
Kevin Jones Associates: 10-11, 38
Joe Lawrence: 5 top, 7, 29 top.
The Maltings Partnership: 4-5, 8-9, 11 top, 12-13, 14-15, 23, 28, 36, 37 bottom, 39, 42-43, 44, 46-47.
Janos Marffy (Kathy Jakeman Illustration): title page, 6-7, 18-19, 26-27, 34-35.
Michael Saunders: 29 bottom, 30-31, 37 top
Mark Stacey: 21.

Editor: Veronica Pennycook
Designers: Mark Summersby and Anne Sharples
Production Controller: Mark Leonard
Picture Researcher: Anna Smith

First published in Great Britain 1995 by Hamlyn Children's Books.
This reprint published 1996 by Heinemann Children's Reference,
Halley Court, Jordan Hill, Oxford, OX2 8EJ, a division
of Reed Educational and Professional Publishing Ltd.

Copyright © 1995 Reed Educational and Professional Publishing Ltd.

All rights reserved. No part of this publication may be reproduced,
stored in a retrieval system, or transmitted, in any form or by any means,
electronic, mechanical, photocopying, recording, or otherwise, without the
prior permission of the copyright holders or a licence permitting restricted
copying in the United Kingdom issued by the Copyright Licensing Agency Ltd,
90 Tottenham Court Road, London W1P 9HE.

ISBN 0 600 58394 5

A CIP catalogue record for this book is available at the British Library.
Books printed and bound by Proost, Belgium. See-through pages printed by SMIC, France.

CONTENTS

THE EARTH IN SPACE 4

INSIDE THE EARTH 6

WANDERING CONTINENTS 8

THE SHAKING CRUST 10

MAKING ROCKS 12

MAKING MORE ROCKS 14

ERUPTION! 16

THE CHANGING LANDSCAPE 18

MAKING YET MORE ROCKS 20

ROCKS FROM LIFE 22

USING THE EARTH'S RICHES 24

THE DARKEST DEPTHS 26

COASTS AND CURRENTS 28

RE-CYCLED WATER 30

EROSION UNDERGROUND 32

UP IN THE SKY 34

WHAT'S THE FORECAST? 36

TROPIC TO POLE 38

RUINING THE LANDSCAPE 40

THE POLLUTED EARTH 42

LOOKING AFTER OUR EARTH 44

THE EARTH IN THE FUTURE 46

INDEX 48

THE EARTH IN SPACE

Long ago, people thought that the Earth was at the centre of everything, and its natural wonders were the work of gods and spirits. In the last three centuries, however, scientists have shown that the Earth is just one tiny part of the Universe. Its shape and structure, its climate and surface features, and its life forms, are all shaped by the processes of nature.

CENTRE OF THE UNIVERSE

In ancient times, people believed that the Earth was stationary, solid and flat, and that it was at the very centre of the Universe. They believed that the Earth had been in existence for ever, and quite probably stretched for ever on all sides. The Sun, Moon and stars were thought to move over the Earth in huge arcs across the sky.

During the Great Age of Exploration, in the 15th century, sailors began travelling across oceans to unknown destinations. Soon the 'New World' of the Americas was added to maps. But map-makers still argued about which way up the Earth was. Turn the page upside-down for a more familiar world view.

ONE OF NINE

The views of modern science show that not one of these ancient beliefs is true. The Earth is not at the centre of everything. It is not still, or flat, or even solid. The Earth is one of nine huge, ball-shaped objects in Space called planets, which move round and round the Sun. The Sun is a fairly typical star, like the hundreds of others we see twinkling in the night sky. But because the Sun is so much closer to the Earth than any other star, it seems huge and blazing.

Sun

Mercury

Venus

Earth

Moon

Mars

Jupiter

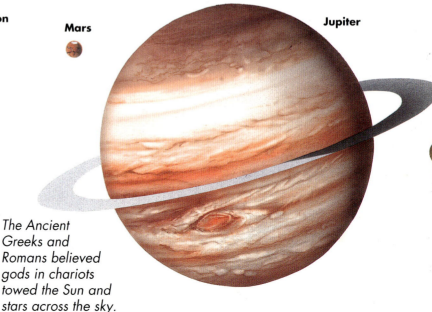

The Ancient Greeks and Romans believed gods in chariots towed the Sun and stars across the sky.

SPINNING LIKE A TOP

The movement of the Earth in Space produces day and night. Our world is spinning around an imaginary line called the axis of rotation. Imagine you are at one spot on its surface. As the Earth turns, your spot comes around to face the Sun. This is morning.

As the Earth continues to turn, you move away from the Sun. This is evening. The Earth takes 24 hours to turn completely on its axis.

Not only does the Earth spin, it also travels around the Sun in an orbit. The orbit of the Earth is not circular but oval, and is called an ellipse. This means that sometimes the Earth is closer to the Sun than at other times. Added to this, the Earth's axis of rotation is tilted compared to the Sun. So some parts of the Earth are closer to or further from the Sun at different times of the year. These variations give us the seasons of summer and winter. When the Earth has completed one orbit, a year has passed.

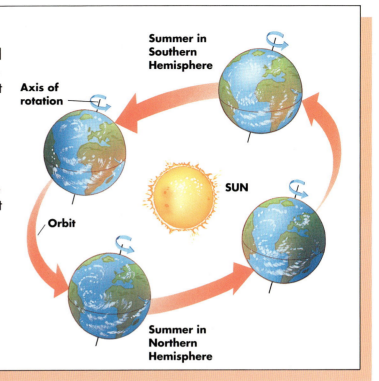

Summer in Southern Hemisphere

Axis of rotation

SUN

Orbit

Summer in Northern Hemisphere

Pluto

Neptune

Uranus

Saturn

The Sun, the nine planets that go around it, and the much smaller moons orbiting some of the planets, all make up our Solar System. The Earth is small compared to most of the planets. But it has a relatively large moon, which we call the Moon. If this diagram was on a realistic scale, with the Earth the size shown here, the Sun would be bigger than a beachball, and the Solar System would fill a soccer pitch!

The Earth goes around the Sun, and the Moon goes around the Earth. When the Moon goes between the Sun and Earth, it blots out our view of the Sun. This is called a solar eclipse. Here, just a tiny part of the Sun is visible.

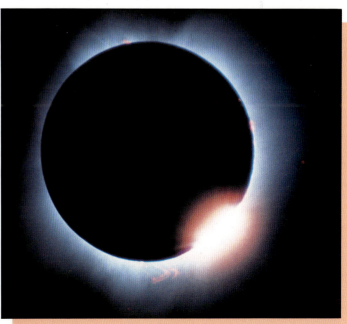

INSIDE THE EARTH

Imagine that you could slice open the Earth like a giant apple. Inside, you would see several layers. The outermost layer is the crust. Inside this is the mantle, then the outer core, and at the centre (like an apple), is the inner core. At least, this is what scientists believe. No one has ever seen these parts. Even the very deepest drill hole is like a tiny pinprick in the crust.

The deepest drill holes only scratch the Earth's surface. The research holes shown in this photo are 20 metres deep. A typical oil well has holes a few hundred metres deep. On land, the deepest borehole is 13,000 metres deep, and in the seabed it is 1,740 metres. At about 12,000 metres down, the temperature is already over twice that of boiling water.

Crust

Inner Core

Outer Core

Mantle

DID YOU KNOW?
The Earth is not a perfectly round sphere. It is slightly flattened at the top and bottom, the North and South Poles. It is also slightly bulging around its middle, the Equator. The distance around the Equator is 40,075 kilometres - it would take 17 days driving non-stop at motorway speed to go around.

A slice out of the Earth reveals the layers deep below the surface. The layers are separated from each other by very thin zones called discontinuities.

BENEATH OUR FEET

As we stand on its surface, we can think of nothing more solid and stationary than the Earth. But deep below our feet, the Earth is not solid. Near its centre it is a slightly runny liquid like very thick treacle. The rock has become molten, or melted into a liquid, because of the intense heat and pressure at the Earth's centre. We know about the deeper parts of the Earth from observing the effects of volcanoes, earthquakes and special explosions.

THE CRUST

The Earth's hard outer layer or 'skin' is called the crust. It is much thinner, in proportion to the whole planet, than the skin of an apple compared to the whole apple. There are two types of crust. Under the main land masses, known as continents, is the continental crust. It varies from 30 to 70 kilometres in thickness. Under the oceans and seas is the oceanic crust, which is about 5 to 10 kilometres thick. Both types of crust are made of solid rock.

THE MANTLE

Under the crust is the thickest layer of the Earth, which is known as the mantle. It is around 2,900 kilometres thick. The mantle is made up chiefly of the chemicals silicon, magnesium, iron and oxygen. The deeper parts of the mantle are flexible, or 'plastic'.

We cannot sense the Earth's magnetism with our own bodies. But many animals probably can, from butterflies to birds and whales. Each year these animals undertake their long-distance journeys, called migrations, and find their way partly by using their natural 'body compass'. Humpback whales migrate thousands of kilometres yearly.

THE CORE

The core has two main layers. The outer core is 2,200 kilometres thick and is made mainly of iron, oxygen and nickel. This layer is red-hot, molten rock that flows slowly. The inner core is a solid ball 2,500 kilometres across, again composed mainly of iron, oxygen and nickel.

As you get nearer to the core, the temperature rises steadily. Only one kilometre down, it is 25-30°C warmer than at the surface. At the core, the temperature reaches an incredible 4,500°C.

THE MAGNETIC EARTH

The slow flow of iron and other substances in the outer core makes the Earth act as a giant magnet. We use this magnetism to find our way with a compass. The compass needle is a thin magnet, which turns to line up with the Earth's magnetism. The needle points to the magnetic North and South Poles. Because of the way the outer core moves, the magnetic North and South Poles are in fact several hundred kilometres from the geographic North and South Poles.

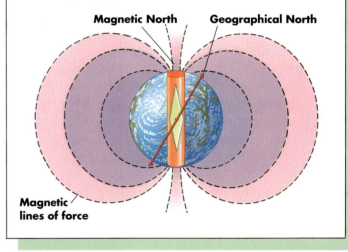

Magnetic North   **Geographical North**

Magnetic lines of force

WANDERING CONTINENTS

The surface of the Earth may seem still, but it is not. The Atlantic Ocean gets wider every year, by about seven centimetres, taking Europe away from North America. Likewise, the Pacific Ocean is becoming narrower. The Himalayan Mountains in Asia are gradually growing higher. All these movements are so slow that we don't notice them taking place. But they have been going on since the Earth began, and will continue far into the future.

MOVING PLATES

Ideas about the Earth's surface have changed enormously in the past 30 years. Scientists now believe that the crust is not a completely solid 'shell' around the Earth, and neither is it still.

The crust is made up of about ten gigantic curved pieces, known as lithospheric plates. There are also another ten or so smaller plates. These plates are slowly drifting around the globe. This means the world map in millions of years will be very different from the map of today.

250 million years ago

150 million years ago

50 million years ago

About 250 million years ago, all of the continents were joined together. They formed a great super-continent called Pangaea. Gradually, they have drifted to the positions we know today. And the drift is still continuing.

Plates collide

As two plates come together, one may simply crash straight into the other. This happens mainly when the continental parts of plates collide. The edges of the plates push and buckle and fold, forming mountains. The Himalayas are forming in this way.

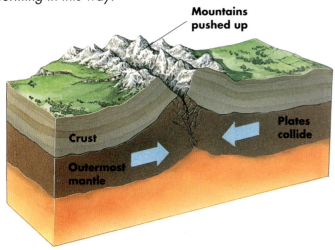

Mountains pushed up

Crust

Plates collide

Outermost mantle

Plates move apart

As two plates move apart, molten rock wells up from below. It cools and goes solid, and adds to the edges of the plates. This happens at plate boundaries under certain seas and the mountains created are called a mid-oceanic ridge.

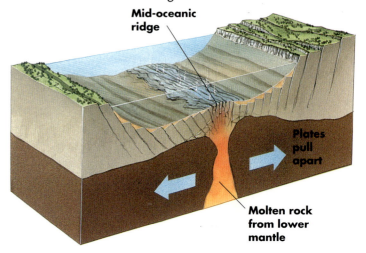

Mid-oceanic ridge

Plates pull apart

Molten rock from lower mantle

Today

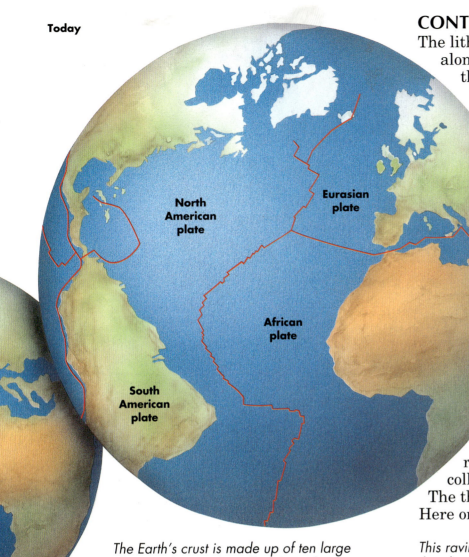

The Earth's crust is made up of ten large plates and several smaller plates that are slowly drifting around the globe.

North American plate

Eurasian plate

African plate

South American plate

CONTINENTAL DRIFT

The lithospheric plates are not sections of crust alone. They also include the outermost part of the mantle underneath. These immense, rigid, curved slabs of rock float on the more flexible mantle beneath.

The plates do not correspond with the actual continents as we see them on a map. Most plates extend out beyond the coastlines of the continents, and under the oceans. So a typical plate is like a raft of rock with a continent embedded in it. As the plate moves, the continent drifts with it. This is the process of continental drift.

ACTION AT THE EDGES

For the lithospheric plates to move, they must change in size and shape. This happens at their edges. There are three types of plate boundary. Where new rock wells up from deep in the Earth, it adds to the edge of a plate. This is a mid-oceanic ridge. At a subduction zone, one plate collides with another or slides down under it. The third boundary is called a transform fault. Here one plate slides past another.

This ravine in Iceland, in the North Atlantic Ocean, marks the place where the North American and Eurasian plates are pulling apart.

Plates slide past

As two plates slide past each other, they rub and grind their edges. Because the edges are not smooth, they may lock together for a while. But then the forces become too great, and the edges suddenly give way and slide many metres. This is an earthquake (see page 10).

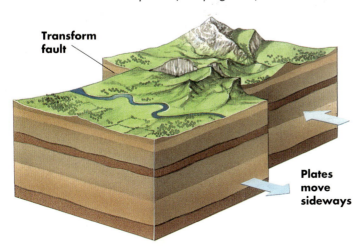

Transform fault

Plates move sideways

THE SHAKING CRUST

It is an ordinary, peaceful day. Suddenly, there is a distant rumbling sound. The ground seems to tremble slightly, then it shudders more violently. Within a few seconds the whole landscape is shaking. Trees and buildings topple over, roads crack, bridges twist and the land gashes open. It is one of nature's most violent events – an earthquake.

In 1989 an earthquake measuring 6.9 on the Richter scale shook south-west California, USA. It was on the San Andreas Fault, part of the boundary between the Pacific and North American plates. The focus was 18 kilometres deep, but it still destroyed houses and other structures.

WAVES OF DESTRUCTION

Most earthquakes happen at the edges of the great lithospheric plates which make up the Earth's surface. Some plates move fairly smoothly, a tiny amount at a time. But other plates stick together until the forces build up, and then they suddenly slip. The result is immense shock waves called seismic waves, that ripple upwards and outwards.

FOCUS AND EPICENTRE

The main place where the two plates push past each other, and where the shaking originates, is called the focus. It is often deep in the crust, many kilometres down. The place on the surface directly above the focus is known as the epicentre. The seismic waves appear to spread out from here. In a powerful earthquake, they can be felt thousands of kilometres away.

DID YOU KNOW?

The strength of earthquakes is measured using the Richter scale, which goes from one to ten. An earthquake of 6.5 or above usually causes damage and destruction. The biggest earthquakes register over 8 on the Richter scale.

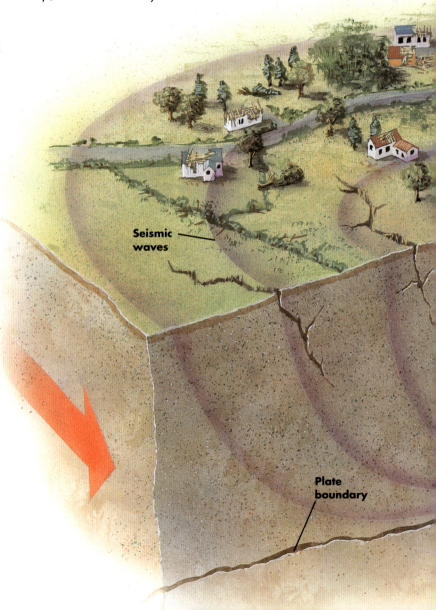

Seismic waves

Plate boundary

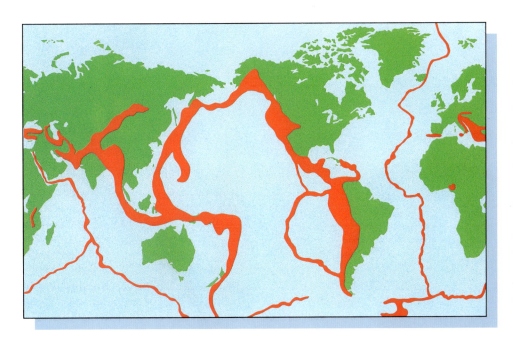

This map shows the main earthquake zones around the world. Compare it with the map of the plates on the previous page. Many quakes happen where the plates slip past or under each other.

MANY TINY QUAKES

Each year there are over 5,000 earthquakes around the world. Nearly all are measured by scientists, but the quakes are usually too small, or in too remote a place, to be noticed by most people.

Only about 500 earthquakes are noticed by people each year. Of these, 50 cause damage. About 10-15 are big enough, or in a populated enough area, to cause loss of life and great damage to buildings, roads, railways, bridges and other structures. Every few years, a powerful earthquake in a populated area makes world news.

A 'tidal wave' is usually the result of an earthquake under the sea. The shocks and vibrations produce huge currents in the water. These spread across the ocean as great waves, called tsunamis. Since many people live around the coasts, tsunamis can cause immense devastation as they surge on to the land.

The shock waves from an earthquake spread out from the central place where the movement is greatest, called the focus. The shaking topples trees and buildings. At fault lines the ground splits, or one part moves vertically to create a cliff or gulley.

Epicentre

Landslip fault

Focus

MAKING ROCKS

Pick up a lump of rock. Compared to you, it is probably very old. It may even be millions of years old. But compared to the age of the Earth, it is probably very young. Rocks have not stayed the same since the Earth began. They are continually being squashed, crushed, heated, melted, worn down and broken up by natural forces. Old rocks become new, different rocks.

CHANGING ROCKS

There are many kinds of rocks, from pure white chalk in high cliffs, to jet black obsidian which shines like glass. Some rocks are very hard and heavy, such as granite. Others, like pumice, are softer and lighter. The rocks in the Earth's crust are always changing, as the minerals in them are recycled into new types of rocks over millions of years.

Black obsidian

White chalk

Coarse granite

These three substances are very different, yet they are all rocks. Chalk is a sedimentary rock, white and powdery. Obsidian and granite are igneous rocks. Obsidian is black and glassy with very sharp edges. Granite is speckled and truly 'rock-hard'.

MINERALS

Minerals are combinations of natural substances. A common example is silica. This is a combination of silicon and oxygen. But we know it better as sand.

Each mineral has its own scientific name. It also has characteristic features such as colour, shininess, hardness, brittleness and so on. There are hundreds of different minerals. They include diamond and ruby, which are extremely precious, and feldspars, which make up vast amounts of rocks but are much less famous!

DID YOU KNOW?

There are hundreds of different kinds of rocks. Each of these features helps to put rocks into categories:
- ◆ Grain size – the size of the particles which make up the rock
- ◆ Opacity – whether the rock is partly see-through
- ◆ Cleavage – the way the rock cracks or breaks
- ◆ Hardness
- ◆ Colour

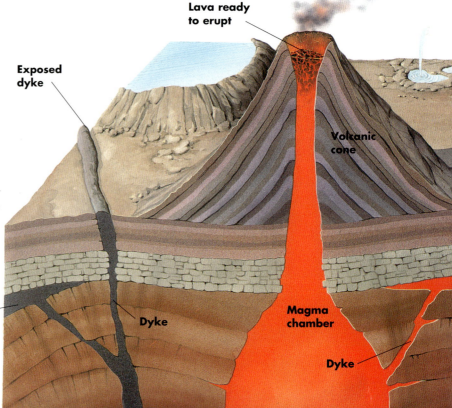

Lava ready to erupt

Exposed dyke

Volcanic cone

Sill

Dyke

Magma chamber

Dyke

THREE TYPES OF ROCKS

Rocks are grouped according to the way they are made. There are three main groups. These are igneous rocks (see below), metamorphic rocks (see page 14) and sedimentary rocks (see page 20).

IGNEOUS ROCKS

Igneous rocks were all once liquid and runny. The original rock melted, and when it cooled and became solid again, it changed its nature.

The heat to melt rock comes from deep below the ground. Molten rock in and under the crust is called magma. If it oozes nearer the crust, the magma may gradually cool and solidify, to form igneous rock. If it reaches the surface, it is called lava. It may flow from a crack or erupt from volcanoes. Again, as the lava cools, it forms igneous rock. Two of the commonest of all rocks, basalt and granite, are igneous rocks.

One of the best-known igneous rocks is basalt. It is dark and has very small grains. It is formed from cooled lava. In some parts of the world, runny rocks have cooled and solidified into great sheets of basalt, hundreds of kilometres across and thousands of metres thick. In other places the lava forms ripples, as on the volcanic island of Hawaii.

Vast amounts of igneous rocks, especially granite, are made when molten rocks cool slowly beneath the surface. These may be huge pools called batholiths, or thinner flat sheets called sills and dykes, which fill the gaps between other rocks.

Granite is a very hard igneous rock often used in building. It is light in colour and has large grains. It usually forms as molten rock cools beneath the surface. Many buildings in Eastern Scotland, like Aberdeen's Town House, are built from granite.

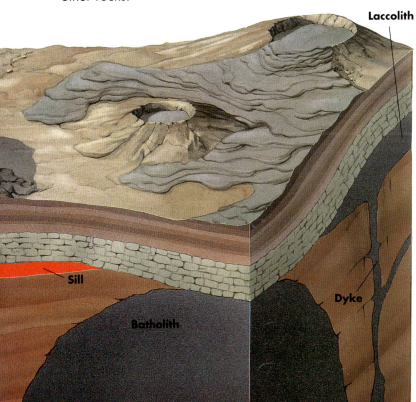

Laccolith

Sill

Batholith

Dyke

◆MAKING MORE ROCKS

Even solid rock cannot survive the tremendous forces generated inside the Earth. When two of the great surface plates meet, they may push into one another so hard that the rock is squashed, crumpled and buckled. The bent rocks fold over and pile up, and form mountains. The incredible pressure and high temperature deep in the ground change the old rocks into new ones.

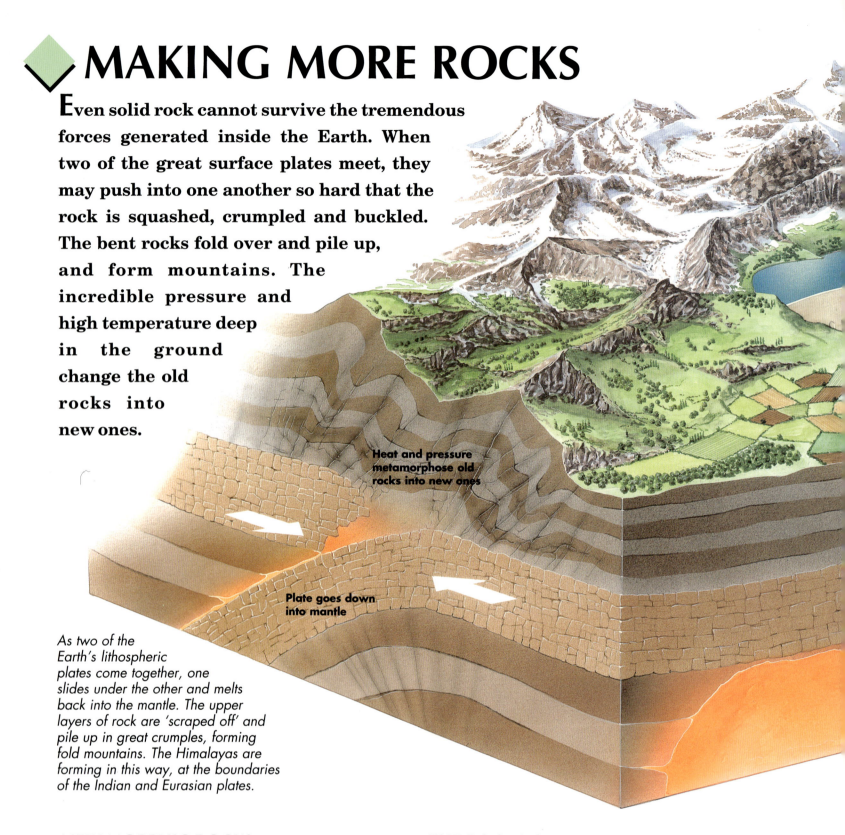

Heat and pressure metamorphose old rocks into new ones

Plate goes down into mantle

As two of the Earth's lithospheric plates come together, one slides under the other and melts back into the mantle. The upper layers of rock are 'scraped off' and pile up in great crumples, forming fold mountains. The Himalayas are forming in this way, at the boundaries of the Indian and Eurasian plates.

METAMORPHIC ROCKS

The second great group of rocks is metamorphic or 'changed' rocks. These are produced from other rocks, called the parent rocks. The intense pressure and heat inside the Earth make the parent rock change chemically and re-form as new rock. The parent rock may get very hot, but it does not melt. If it did, the result would be an igneous rock (see pages 12-13).

THE ROOTS OF THE MOUNTAINS

Mountains can be built in several ways. One is by volcanic eruption (see pages 16-17). Another way is through the collision of two lithospheric plates. As this happens, the enormous pressures from the sides, and from thousands of metres of rock above, squashes the parent rock hard. The minerals change and rearrange themselves into new types of metamorphic rocks.

THE HIGHEST MOUNTAINS

The Himalayas are by far the tallest mountains in the world, with all of the top ten peaks. The tallest mountains on each continent or region are:

Name	Place	Height (metres)
Everest	Himalayas, Asia	8,848
Aconcagua	Andes, South America	6,959
McKinley	Alaska, North America	6,194
Kilimanjaro	East Africa	5,895
Vinson	Antarctica	5,140
Blanc	Alps, Europe	4,807
Wilhelm	Papua New Guinea, SE Asia	4,509
Elbert	Rockies, North America	4,399
Cook	New Zealand	3,764
Kosciusko	Australia	2,229
Ben Nevis	Scotland	1,343

METAMORPHIC ROCK

Some of the most useful and beautiful rocks are metamorphic. Slate is one. It has been quarried for hundreds of years, to make roofing tiles, table tops, shelves and hearths. It is also used for the bases of snooker and pool tables and it was the original blackboard for writing on with chalk.

Marble is another metamorphic rock. It can be cut or chiselled in almost any direction, and its beautiful swirls and sheens make it a prized material for statues and sculptures. It is also used to decorate buildings and for columns and floor tiles.

Abandoned slate quarry

Marble statue

The Alps are the largest mountain system in Europe. They have been formed by folding, and are still fairly young at just a few million years old. Their sharp, jagged peaks have not yet been rounded and worn down.

◆ERUPTION!

Volcanoes are formed when molten rock flows out through an opening in the Earth's crust. Most volcanoes occur at a weak spot in the crust, usually between two great plates.

TYPES OF VOLCANO

The molten rock can ooze out slowly, or burst out like a fountain. Very hot, thin, runny lava forms a low, wide mountain called a shield volcano. The lava runs down the volcano's sides like syrup, and gradually cools and hardens. Thicker lava forms a round hill called a dome volcano. Very thick, stiff lava flows slowly and piles up to form a cone volcano.

HOW VOLCANOES FORM

Deep below the ground, pressure builds up around the magma, until it forces its way up through the volcano and out of a hole, or vent. If the magma is very thick, the pressure can be so great that the lava bursts out with a deafening roar, spreading smoke, gases, jets of ash and solid lumps of rock called volcanic bombs.

The lava makes its way up a tunnel called a shaft, or conduit, from the magma chamber deep below. It oozes down the sides of the volcano, and then cools and goes solid, forming new streams and waves of rock. Each eruption adds another layer of lava, and so the volcano grows taller.

Cracks in the volcano's sides allow more lava to seep out, forming smaller volcanoes on the main cone called parasitic cones.

YEARS LATER

Volcanoes do not last for ever. Sometimes they go quiet and are said to be dormant. In this state, they may erupt again, at any moment. Then finally, the magma below cools and the volcano dies, or becomes extinct.

The outer layers of rock will gradually wear away, and mix into soil. Plants and animals may spread over the fertile slopes. The central shaft inside an old volcano is filled with magma that has solidified into very hard rock. Over time, the rest of the volcano wears away, but it often leaves the hard central rock sticking up as a volcanic plug. In some volcanoes, an explosive eruption blasts away this central rock leaving a crater which becomes filled with water, known as a crater lake.

Somewhere, a new volcano will be bursting into life, showing the awesome power of the Earth's natural forces.

INSIDE VOLCANOES

1   Dome volcano
2   Shield volcano
3   Cone volcano
4   Main vent
5   Main shaft or conduit
6   Magma chamber
7   Layers of lava from earlier eruptions
8   Side vent
9   Parasitic cone
10   A dyke is a sheet of hardened lava from an earlier explosion.
11   Crater lake
12   Volcanic plug
13   An extinct volcano provides fertile land for farming.

THE CHANGING LANDSCAPE

If you could come back to your home area in 10,000 years, you'd notice many changes. Of course, the buildings and roads would be different. But the hills and valleys would also have changed. Some parts might be lifted higher by the immense forces which shape the rocks of the crust. Other areas might be worn lower, by the never-ending effects of Sun, wind, rain and ice.

Windblown sand has eroded these limestone spires in the Australian desert.

WEATHERING

Have you ever left a favourite toy outside for a long time? The weather soon has its effects. Hot, sunny summer days are followed by the cold, freezing times of winter. The toy fades, cracks and rots away.

The same happens to rocks, only much more slowly. Rocks are hard and strong. Yet over thousands of years, they too are gradually worn away by the weather. This process is called weathering.

TEMPERATURE

The hot Sun shines down, and rocks absorb its heat. They get bigger, or expand. When the Sun sets, the rocks cool and get smaller, or contract. The continual cycle of expansion and contraction makes the surface of the rock crack. Tiny bits fall off, and so the rock gets smaller.

RAIN, FROST AND ICE

The rain also beats down and wears away the surface of the rocks. Natural rainwater often contains tiny amounts of substances from the air that turn it into a very weak acid (see page 43). This affects certain rocks chemically, and dissolves them away. Modern air pollution makes the rain much more acid, and speeds up the process.

In cold weather, rain freezes into ice. As it does so, it expands. When water seeps into tiny cracks in the rock, and then freezes, it pushes the cracks wider. This is called frost wedging, and it makes pieces of rock split and fall off.

WIND AND WATER

Wind, by itself, has little effect on rocks. But it often carries dust, sand and other particles. When these are blown at a rock, they scratch it, blasting tiny fragments from the rock's surface.

Running water has the same effect. A stream rolls and tumbles pebbles, wearing away its bed. Waterfalls and rapids do the same. So do waves on the shore, as they crash against the rocks. So do rockfalls and avalanches tumbling down a mountain. So do glaciers. This type of wear, when particles rub and scrape and scratch, is called erosion.

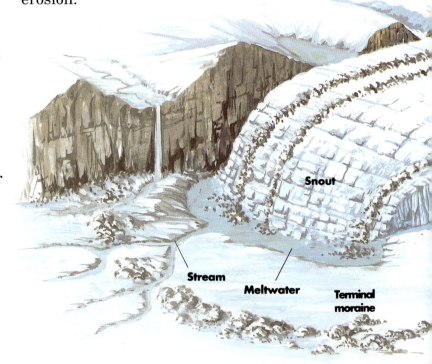

Snout

Stream

Meltwater

Terminal moraine

In some cold places, snow falls faster than it melts. The snow collects in valleys, gets squashed and turns to ice. The ice is solid, but it 'flows' downhill very slowly, as a river of ice called a glacier. The ice picks up stones and boulders and carries them along as moraines. These stones scrape the rocks, wearing them away to form a U-shaped valley. Glaciers have very powerful erosive action.

Side glacier

Compacted snow

Medial moraine

Lateral moraine

Fast-flowing water carrying pebbles has eroded this deep gorge in France.

When plants find a good place to grow, they send out anchoring roots. The roots are small, but they grow steadily. They can crack paths and roads, and even topple buildings. This photo shows tree roots gradually destroying a stone wall. The same happens in the landscape, as roots split rocks, helping with the weathering process.

19

MAKING YET MORE ROCKS

Where do the little bits of worn-away hills and mountains go? Most of them are swept along by the rain, into streams and rivers. They are carried down into lakes and seas, where they settle on the bottom. This is the first stage in a long process that makes the third main type of rock.

SEDIMENTARY ROCKS

The particles which result from weathering and erosion vary from tiny specks, which are too small to see, to large cobbles and boulders. These particles are washed along by running water, or blown along by the wind. Eventually, somewhere, they come to rest. The larger ones may settle on a river bed. The smaller ones are lighter and get carried further. They float down the river, out through the estuary, or river-mouth, and into a lake or sea.

These sandstone rocks in Utah, USA, have been eroded to form a tall cliff. This shows how sedimentary rocks form in layers, or beds. The topmost layers are 10 million years old. The lowest are 150 million years old and have dinosaur footprints in them.

PARTICLE SIZE

When studying rocks, everyday terms like 'sand' or 'mud' have very specific meanings. The main factor is the average size of the bits or particles.

Name	Particle size (millimetres)
Clay	smaller than 0.004 mm
Silt	0.004 to 0.06 mm
Sand	0.06 to 2 mm
Gravel (granule)	2 to 4 mm
Pebble	4 to 64 mm
Cobble	64 to 256 mm
Boulder	larger than 256 mm

SETTLING OUT

Eventually, the particles sink to the bottom. Since weathering and erosion are always happening, more and more particles follow them. They pile up into layers called sediments.

Some sediments are mixed, with particles of many different sizes. But often the particles in a particular place are all of a similar size. They have been naturally sorted, or graded, by the effects of wind or water currents.

SQUEEZED AND CEMENTED

Gradually, the layers of sediments get deeper. The ones at the bottom are pressed by the weight of those on top. Slowly, the separate particles are squeezed, and become glued or cemented together. After thousands or millions of years, they have formed solid rocks.

SHALES AND SANDSTONES

There are various kinds of sedimentary rocks. They depend on the parent rocks which the original particles came from, how big the bits are, and what cements them together. The most common are shales, which are basically hardened mud. The particles in shales are tiny, and visible only under a microscope. The next most common are sandstones and limestones.

Conglomerates are sedimentary rocks formed from cemented gravel or pebbles. They have large rounded particles, easily seen by the unaided eye. The particles have been worn smooth by rolling and tumbling along a river bed. This is a mixed conglomerate from Hertfordshire, England.

Sandstone blocks are frequently used for buildings.

Breccias are sedimentary rocks where the particles are large and sharp-edged. They were freshly broken from their parent rock, and were not worn round and smooth, like those in conglomerates. The quartz pieces in this breccia are cemented together by a dark red mineral called groundmass.

Flint is a very hard sedimentary rock that cracks into sharp-edged pieces. Stone-age people chipped it into tools such as axes, scrapers, spearheads and knives. Flint gives a spark when struck hard, so it was used to set off the gunpowder in cannons and old-fashioned flintlock pistols. This is a cracked lump or nodule of flint.

ROCKS FROM LIFE

Millions of years ago, the last dinosaurs lay dying by a river. What killed them? No one is sure. But their flesh rotted, and their bones were washed along the river and into the sea. They sank to the bottom, and got stuck in the sediments. Gradually, the land buckled and rose, due to great earth movements, and formed mountains. The rocks over the bones eroded away.

Rock

Coiled shell

These fossils are the coiled shells of ammonoids, sea creatures resembling squids that lived 200 million years ago.

FOSSILS

Fossils are the remains of animals and plants which died long ago. Their body parts were trapped in the rocks and turned to stone.

Most fossils are of the hard parts, such as the bones, teeth, claws, horns, scales and shells of animals, and the bark, stems, seeds, nuts and cones of plants. The softer parts, such as the skin and muscles of animals, or the leaves and petals of plants, rotted away too quickly to be preserved. Or they got eaten by scavengers.

BONE TO STONE

Fossils are found in sedimentary rocks. The bones and other remains were turned to stone as part of the rock-making process, as they and the particles around them were squeezed and cemented. In general, it takes tens of thousands of years for the remains of living things to become fossils.

Fossils hardly ever occur in igneous and metamorphic rocks. The melting, heat and pressure destroy the original fossil shapes.

THE STORY OF LIFE ON EARTH

Fossils are fascinating, because they tell us about the kinds of animals and plants that lived on the Earth in prehistoric times. Because of the way that sedimentary rocks form, the oldest layers are usually at the bottom. By examining the fossils, we can see how life has evolved.

FOSSIL ROCKS

The most spectacular fossils are of giant dinosaurs, huge fishes and enormous trees. But tiny animals and plants also formed fossils. Indeed, these tiny organisms were so numerous, especially in the seas, that some types of sedimentary rocks consist almost entirely of their fossilized remains.

A palaeontologist, or fossil expert, carefully chips away sedimentary rocks to reveal the remains of a large dinosaur. Its preserved tail bones are at the top, with a long, curved rib on the left. Studying fossils provides us with a lot of information about early life on Earth.

22

FOSSIL FUELS

Much of the energy we use is provided by oil, coal and gas. These are fossil fuels – they have all formed from the remains of animals and plants buried deep under the surface.

MAKING COAL

Coal is the partly rotted and fossilized remains of giant plants such as tree ferns, which flourished on Earth millions of years ago. First, the remains are pressed into peat, and then they become a light brown rock called lignite. They are squashed further into coal, and perhaps metamorphosed, or changed, into a dense black type of coal called anthracite. Most coal comes from plants which lived around 300 million years ago.

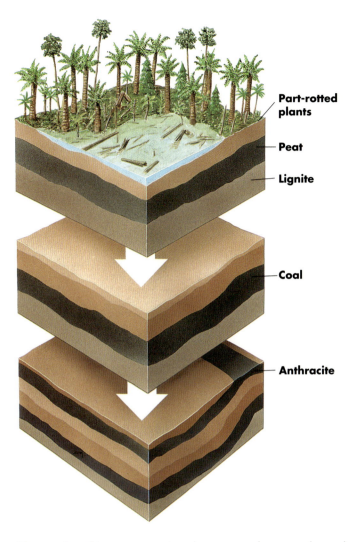

- Part-rotted plants
- Peat
- Lignite
- Coal
- Anthracite

The coal making process involves several stages that take millions of years to complete. At each stage, the substance can be burned, but the older and more rock-like it is, the better it burns. So peat gives the least heat, and anthracite the most.

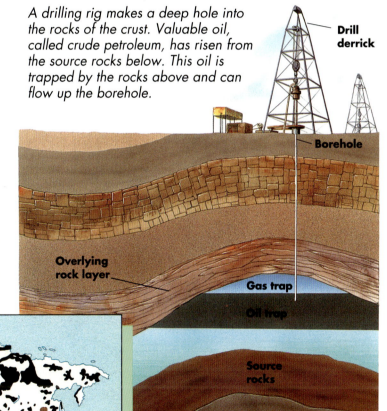

A drilling rig makes a deep hole into the rocks of the crust. Valuable oil, called crude petroleum, has risen from the source rocks below. This oil is trapped by the rocks above and can flow up the borehole.

- Drill derrick
- Borehole
- Overlying rock layer
- Gas trap
- Oil trap
- Source rocks

Coal field   Oil field

Coal and oil are valuable fuels and raw materials. This map shows the main coal and oil fields around the world. New ones are occasionally discovered. But we are using up our reserves of coal and oil millions of times faster than they can re-form.

◆ USING THE EARTH'S RICHES

Next time you walk in the countryside or visit the seaside, go to a high place and look out over the scene before you. It may seem peaceful, with people rambling through the woods, or sunbathing on the beach. But look again, and you might see clues to the way we are using up the riches of our planet.

MINES AND QUARRIES

On the land, there may be the scars of quarries. You might feel a deep boom from the quarry as explosives blast and loosen rock. Diggers and cranes then scoop out valuable rocks, ores and minerals. Only small amounts of rock are used. The rest is leftover waste, piled into huge heaps.

Tall pit-head buildings mean there are mines deep underground. The miners dig out coal and other minerals, ore rocks for metals, and even gold or diamonds. The mine tunnels may reach right under the sea.

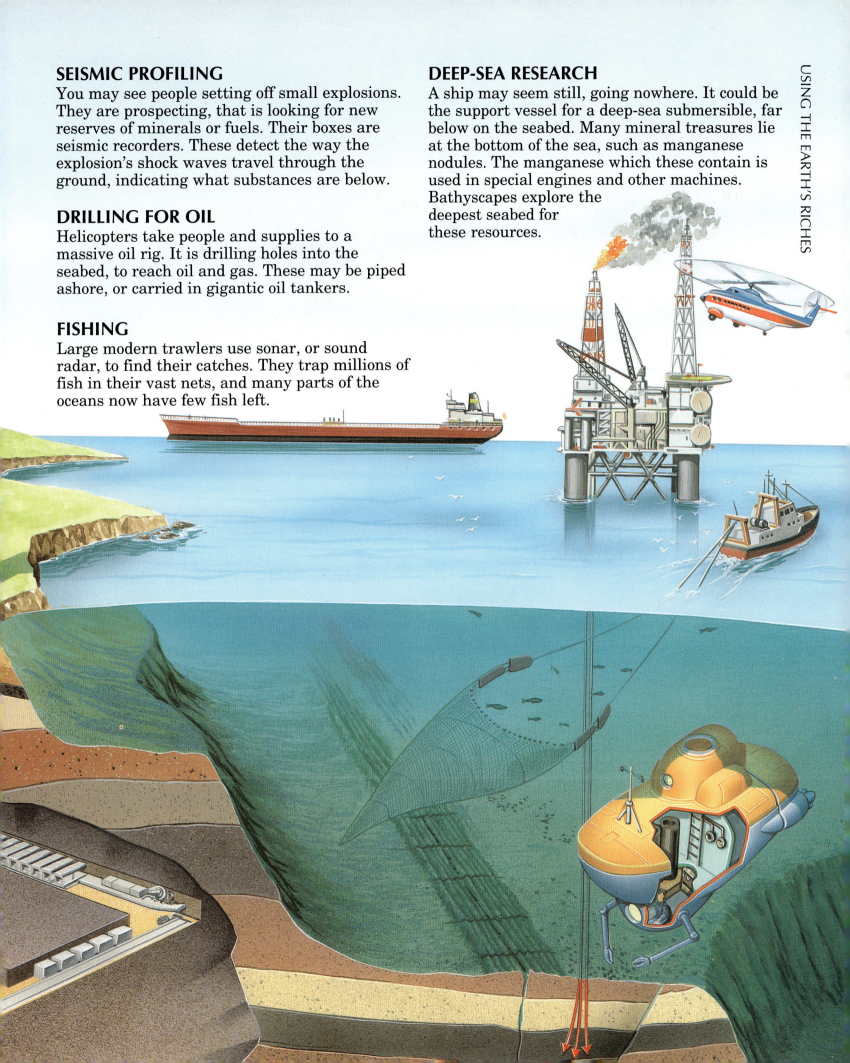

SEISMIC PROFILING

You may see people setting off small explosions. They are prospecting, that is looking for new reserves of minerals or fuels. Their boxes are seismic recorders. These detect the way the explosion's shock waves travel through the ground, indicating what substances are below.

DRILLING FOR OIL

Helicopters take people and supplies to a massive oil rig. It is drilling holes into the seabed, to reach oil and gas. These may be piped ashore, or carried in gigantic oil tankers.

FISHING

Large modern trawlers use sonar, or sound radar, to find their catches. They trap millions of fish in their vast nets, and many parts of the oceans now have few fish left.

DEEP-SEA RESEARCH

A ship may seem still, going nowhere. It could be the support vessel for a deep-sea submersible, far below on the seabed. Many mineral treasures lie at the bottom of the sea, such as manganese nodules. The manganese which these contain is used in special engines and other machines. Bathyscapes explore the deepest seabed for these resources.

THE DARKEST DEPTHS

Around the edges of most continents, the sea is only 200-300 metres deep. These areas are called continental shelves. The water is sunlit and relatively warm here, and many plants and creatures can thrive. Beyond the continental shelves, the seabed plunges down thousands of metres. The permanent darkness of the deep sea is the last unexplored region of our planet.

DARK AND COLD

Salt water covers more than two-thirds of our globe. And this vast expanse of sea is very deep. Some six-sevenths of the oceans and seas are deeper than 500 metres.

Sunlight does not go down that far, so the water is pitch black and cold. No plants grow. But strange animals live there, surviving on the 'rain' of food particles, dead bodies and droppings which drift down from the brighter, warmer surface waters.

THE DEEPEST OF THE DEEP

Each ocean has several cliff-sided valleys in its floor which plunge to incredible depths. These are the ocean trenches, the deepest places on Earth. They are usually the sites of subduction zones (see page 9), where the edge of one great lithospheric plate dips below another, into the mantle beneath.

Name	Ocean	Depth (metres)
Marianas	West Pacific	11,034
Tonga	South Pacific	10,800
Puerto Rico	North Mid-Atlantic	8,412
South Sandwich	South Atlantic	8,263
Aleutian	East Pacific	8,100
Weber	Indian	7,258

If you could travel high in a spacecraft, and look below the surface of the ocean, you might get this see-through view of the sea floor. Most sea life is clustered around the shores and shallow waters near the land, and in the top 500 metres or so of the open ocean.

DEEP-SEA CREATURES

The deep-sea sea-lily is not a flower. It is an animal that lives anchored to the seabed by a stiff stalk

The gulper eel is mostly mouth. It is designed to swallow almost any meal that it encounters.

The sperm whale descends more than 2,000 metres and is the deepest-diving of all whales.

Submarine using sonar to explore the ocean floor

Tips of mid-oceanic volcanoes break the surface as small islands, often in a chain

Magma conduits

THE SEASCAPE

The deep seabed is made up of immense, flat, mud-covered plains, mountain chains and cliff-sided trenches. These are all much larger than similar structures on land. The undersea mountain chains and ridges mostly mark the edges of the great lithospheric plates, where new sea floor is being made (see page 8).

MAPPING THE DEEP

Only a tiny portion of the deep ocean floor has been seen by people. But it has all been mapped, mainly by the technique of sonar. A ship sails across the ocean, beaming out sound waves from an underwater loudspeaker. The sound travels well through the water. It bounces off the seabed and an underwater microphone detects the echoes. A computer works out how far the sounds have travelled, and so shows the depth of the sea and the contours of the seabed.

FAR FROM THE SUN

Not all deep-sea life survives on food drifting down from above. Some have food from below. At certain places, warm water laden with energy-rich sulphur chemicals bubbles up from deep in the Earth, through holes or cracks in the seabed called deep-sea vents. The chemicals in this water feed tiny microbes, which in turn feed unique kinds of tubeworms, mussels, clams, crabs and other deep-sea animal species. These communities, clustered around their deep-sea vents, are the only life on Earth which does not depend ultimately on the Sun.

The continental shelf may extend just a few kilometres from the shore line, or it may go on for over 100 kilometres. The average depth of all the continental shelf areas in the world is 130 metres. Beyond, the continental slope goes down to the abyssal region of deep water.

New sea floor forms along the mid-oceanic ridge

Plate moves sideways

Plate moves sideways

Continental slope

Continental shelf

Coastline

Abyssal plain

Deepsea vent

Oceanic trench

Plate goes down

Magma

OCEANIC CRUST

CONTINENTAL CRUST

COASTS AND CURRENTS

The seaside is a good place to swim and play. It is also an excellent example of erosion at work. The sea wears away the land as the waves crash on to the shore, tossing sand, pebbles and boulders. Yet, in other areas, the sea adds to the land by depositing piles of shingle, sand and mud. These are gradually covered by coastal plants, and become dry land. Even more than other landscapes, the coastline is constantly changing.

WIND AND WAVES

As the Earth spins once each day on its axis, and goes around the Sun once each year, the Sun's heat warms different parts of the Earth's surface by different amounts. Warmed air rises, and cooler air moves along to take its place. This causes winds.

The winds blowing across the ocean whip up waves. Out at sea, the waves are long and rolling. As they reach the shallower water of the shore, waves build up in height, topple over and 'break', crashing on to the coast with enormous power. This action wears away the coast, year after year.

Waves hitting a headland gradually wear it away, forming a coastal arch. Often, the rock of the arch collapses, leaving a column, or 'stack', as shown here.

Waves swish and roll tiny sand grains on to the beach. This continuous movement wears away or adds to the coastline.

OCEAN CURRENTS

Since the Sun heats the Earth unevenly, some patches of ocean are warmed more than others. This sets up ocean currents. Incredible volumes of water circulate around the world. Near land, the shape of the coast affects the major currents so that there are many smaller, local currents. These drag sand and mud around, washing it out to sea or dumping it on to the coast.

The features of the shoreline are fashioned by a combination of many factors, such as the land's rock hardness, and the direction of the main winds, waves and currents.

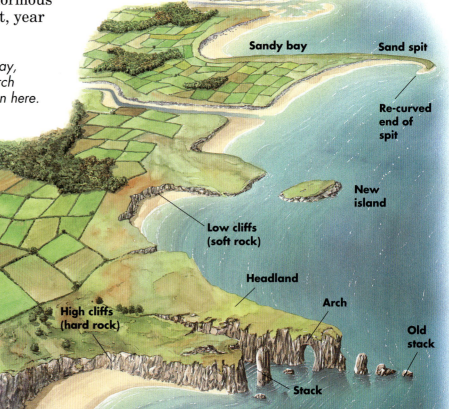

Sandy bay

Sand spit

Re-curved end of spit

New island

Low cliffs (soft rock)

Headland

Arch

Old stack

High cliffs (hard rock)

Stack

THE TIDES

The Moon has a pull, or gravity, like the Earth, although it is less powerful. But the Moon is so close that its gravity affects the Earth. It attracts the water in the seas and oceans, forming a 'bulge'. As the Earth spins in Space and the Moon orbits the Earth, this bulge follows the Moon. The result is the tides, as the sea's surface rises and falls in a cycle lasting about 12 hours 25 minutes. The Sun's gravity is less than the Moon's, but it also affects the tides.

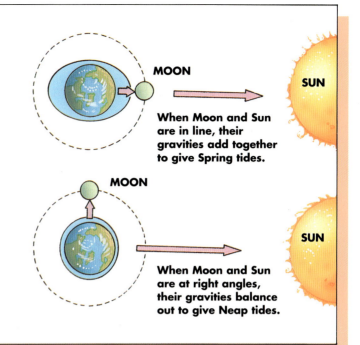

MOON

SUN

When Moon and Sun are in line, their gravities add together to give Spring tides.

MOON

SUN

When Moon and Sun are at right angles, their gravities balance out to give Neap tides.

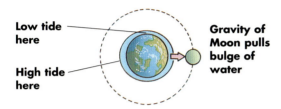

Low tide here

High tide here

Gravity of Moon pulls bulge of water

PROTECTING THE COASTS

Over one-third of all the people in the world live in low-lying areas, on or near the coasts of oceans, seas and lakes. So it is very important to stop the water breaking through and flooding the land. There are several methods of protecting the coasts, such as groynes, or breakwaters. However, the power of the sea is relentless and coastal defences always need repairing and renewing.

The reflector wall changes the direction of waves. Its curved design pushes them back out, so reducing their effects.

Large boulders, or shaped pieces of concrete such as tetrapods, can be piled up at intervals along the shore. They save the beach from the worst of the waves.

The tides are due to the movements of vast amounts of water. This is an energy source which can be harnessed by converting the tidal movement to electricity at a tidal power station. The world's first tidal power station was built at the mouth of the River Rance in Brittany, France. However, it has unfortunately affected the flow of the river, and the places where some animals and plants live.

RE-CYCLED WATER

Have you ever felt really thirsty, with a dry mouth, and just dying for a drink? This shows how vital water is for life. All animals and plants depend on water. And so do many of the forces that shape the Earth's landscapes. Water moves around the planet in many different forms, such as clouds, rain, snow and ice, in living things, in rivers and lakes, and, of course, in the seas and oceans. Yet this is all the same water, going round and round.

Water trickles down cracks into the rocks, and it is also produced from magma cooling far below. If the deep rocks are hot, they boil the water into steam. The pressure builds up, until the steam and water burst from a hole like a fountain, called a geyser. There are many geysers in Iceland and New Zealand.

The most obvious parts of the water cycle are floating clouds, falling rain and snow, rushing rivers and brooks, and wide lakes and seas. Water vapour is also part of the water cycle and it too is moving about, although it is invisible. The ice in glaciers moves as well, but very slowly.

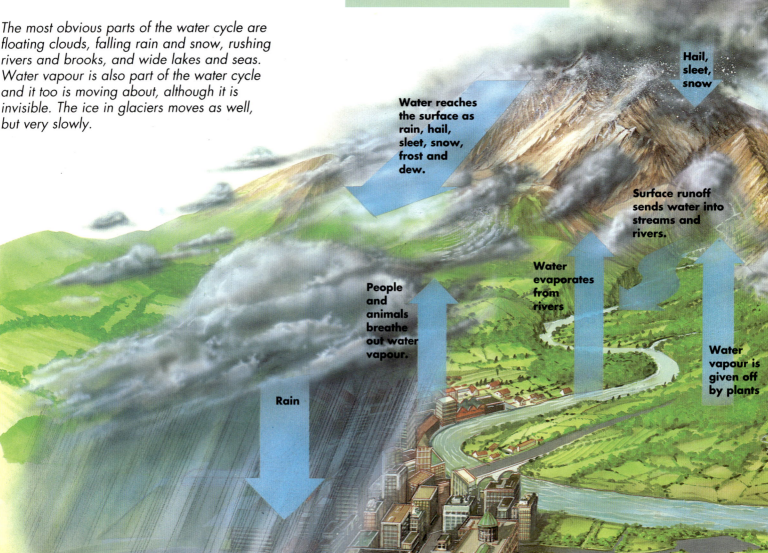

Hail, sleet, snow

Water reaches the surface as rain, hail, sleet, snow, frost and dew.

Surface runoff sends water into streams and rivers.

People and animals breathe out water vapour.

Water evaporates from rivers

Water vapour is given off by plants

Rain

ANCIENT WATER

In nature, new water is hardly ever made, or old water destroyed. The water we have today has been here for millions of years. It merely moves from place to place, in its three main forms. These are the gas called water vapour, the familiar liquid water, and solid water or ice.

This continual movement of water is sometimes called the water cycle. It is really the water re-cycle, as the same water is used again and again.

THE POWER OF THE SUN

The energy that drives the water cycle comes from the Sun. When the Sun comes out after a rainstorm, watch a puddle dry and disappear. The liquid water is warmed by the Sun's heat. It turns into water vapour, which is invisible, and floats up into the air. This process is known as evaporation.

RISING WATER

Evaporation from lakes and seas happens all over the world. The Sun heats the water and produces massive amounts of water vapour. This rises into the air. However, the higher it goes, the colder it gets. The water vapour cools and condenses, or turns back into liquid water. This is usually in the form of tiny water droplets, which float and form clouds (see page 37).

FALLING WATER

Gradually, the water droplets in a cloud get bigger and join together. They become heavier, and fall back to the ground as rain. This trickles over the ground, runs into streams and rivers, and flows into lakes and seas. The Sun's warmth evaporates the water, and the main part of the cycle is complete. However there are many other paths which water can take, as shown in the main picture here.

Water wears away the land in many different ways. Where a river bends, the faster-flowing water on the outside of the bend eats into the bank. This makes the river curve even more. A long bend like this is called a meander. Depending on the hardness of the underlying rocks, the bend may get cut off as the main river takes a new, straighter path again. The isolated water is called an oxbow lake, shown here on the upper left.

Water vapour rises in the atmosphere and cools to form clouds.

Water evaporates from lakes

Underground water rises at springs

The Sun warms any body of water and turns some of it into water vapour.

EROSION UNDERGROUND

Limestone countryside is often rocky, with jagged, stony outcrops and little soil and plants. This is because rainwater drains quickly through the cracks and crevices in the ground, washing away soil and leaving the surface dry and bare. A weak acid in the rain slowly eats away the rock, creating a dark, hidden world of caves.

A CAVE SYSTEM

The rainwater vanishes down a swallowhole and into the rocks below. There, the water turns small cracks into big ones, and little holes into giant caverns. It creates a whole system of caves, tunnels, streams and waterfalls.

After thousands of years, the underground river wears away a huge cavern. When the river discovers a new direction, a dry, dark gallery is left where the river once flowed. A vertical shaft called a chimney was worn away by the gushing water of a now-gone waterfall.

STRANGE FORMATIONS

Centuries of water dripping from the cave roof leave behind tiny traces of minerals. These build up into a stalactite - an 'icicle of rock'. On the ground below the drips, stalagmites grow upwards in a similar way. Over thousands of years, a stalactite and stalagmite may join, forming a pillar.

CAVE LIFE

There are animals in the caves living on bits of food washed in by the water. They need no eyes in their pitch-dark world. Bats fly in to rest by day, hanging from the roof. They emerge at night to feed. Cave insects such as cockroaches and beetles feed on the huge piles of bat droppings. Blind fish live in the dark underground lakes.

INSIDE LIMESTONE CAVES

1	Swallowhole
2	Pothole (dry swallowhole)
3	Underground river
4	Underground waterfall
5	Cavern
6	Gallery
7	Chimney
8	Stalactites
9	Stalagmites
10	Pillar
11	Underground lake
12	Resurgence (river re-emerges)
13	Tourist centre
14	Tourist entrance
15	Cavers exploring cave system

UP IN THE SKY

Imagine gazing from a high hilltop over the countryside. On a bright day you can see for miles. The air is clear and seems completely empty. But air is not empty. It is a mixture of gases made up of tiny molecules that are far too small to see. Normally, air is completely see-through, or transparent. But local weather conditions may mean that the air contains tiny floating dust particles, or droplets of water. This makes the atmosphere hazy or misty, and spoils the beautiful view.

THE ATMOSPHERE

We live in, breathe and move through a layer of air which surrounds the entire Earth. This layer is called the atmosphere. It is held close to the ground by the Earth's pull of gravity. Otherwise, the planet's spinning motion would make the air fly off into Space.

Compared to the size of the whole Earth, the atmosphere is extremely thin – like a layer of clingfilm around a beachball.

AIR FOR LIFE

We breathe air every few seconds. Air is vital for life. Or, rather, it is the gas oxygen which is vital. Oxygen forms about one-fifth of air. Our bodies and those of other animals, and plants too, all need oxygen. Without regular oxygen supplies, nearly all life would cease.

AIR PRESSURE

Air is not weightless. Like any substance, it has weight, though compared to most things, it is very light. As you stand on the ground, there is a column of air above your head, many kilometres high. This presses down with a force called atmospheric pressure. It is equivalent to about one kilogram per square centimetre – which is like a large bag of flour pressing down on every thumbnail-sized patch of your skin, all over your body. You are born into this air pressure and live in it all your life, so you do not notice it.

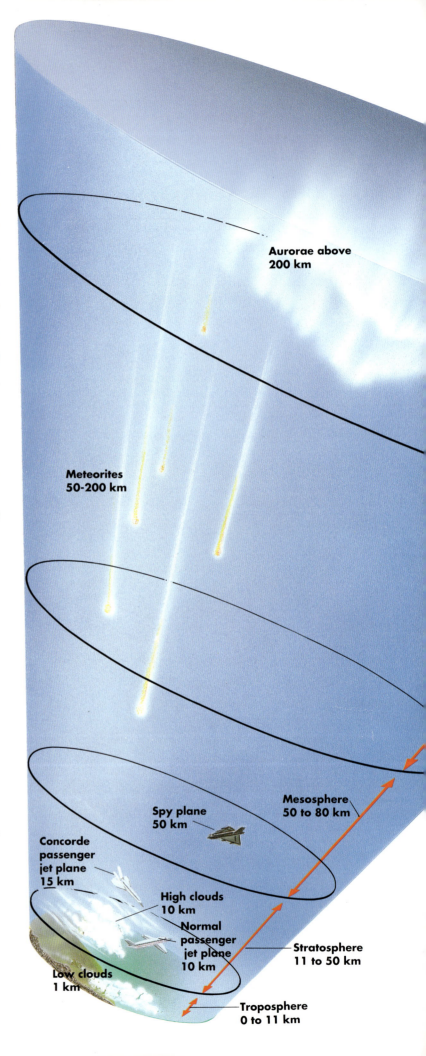

Aurorae above 200 km

Meteorites 50-200 km

Spy plane 50 km

Mesosphere 50 to 80 km

Concorde passenger jet plane 15 km

High clouds 10 km

Normal passenger jet plane 10 km

Stratosphere 11 to 50 km

Low clouds 1 km

Troposphere 0 to 11 km

The atmosphere is divided into four layers, according to the temperature. Yet this does not fall steadily with height. It becomes colder in the troposphere, and then slightly warmer again in the stratosphere, at back up to about 10°C. Then it gets much colder in the mesosphere, down to minus 120°C, and finally warmer again in the thermosphere.

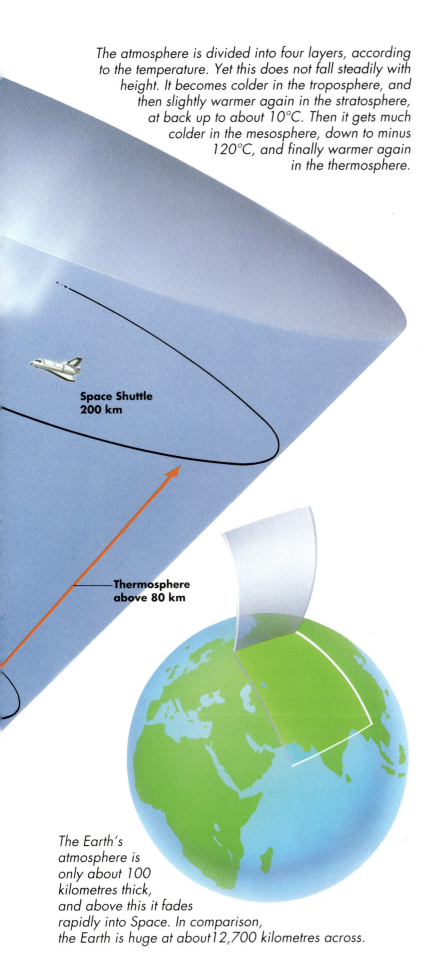

Space Shuttle 200 km

Thermosphere above 80 km

The Earth's atmosphere is only about 100 kilometres thick, and above this it fades rapidly into Space. In comparison, the Earth is huge at about 12,700 kilometres across.

On high mountains, the air is very thin and the body cannot breathe in enough oxygen for its needs. Climbers take oxygen with them in pressure tanks, and breathe it through a tube and face mask.

FADING INTO SPACE

◆ At 10 kilometres high, the air pressure is one-twentieth its amount on the ground.
◆ At 100 kilometres high, the air pressure is almost nothing.
◆ At 700 kilometres, there is no proper air. The atmosphere has faded into the vacuum or nothingness of Space.

THICK TO THIN

The atmosphere is densest, or thickest, at ground level. As you go higher, up a mountain or in an aircraft, the air becomes less dense, or thinner. It also becomes rapidly colder.

If you fly high in a large passenger aircraft, you do not notice these changes. You are sealed into the cabin, and the air pressure and temperature inside are kept the same as they are near the ground. But if you fly high in an open craft like a balloon, you would soon notice the changes. You would begin to feel cold and to shiver. You would gasp for breath as oxygen became more scarce.

35

WHAT'S THE FORECAST ?

What's the weather like today? If you are indoors, you may not notice. But if you work or play outside, then the weather is much more important. These days, forecasting the weather is a complicated process that produces valuable information. It affects the daily lives of farmers, aircraft pilots, ship captains, gardeners and many others.

This map shows the major wind patterns around the world. They change with the seasons, and are also affected by ocean currents. They are especially important for aircraft. A following wind can shorten a long-haul plane journey by one or two hours, saving fuel as well as time.

WHAT'S IN THE WEATHER?

The weather affects us all. It can change daily or even by the minute, and it is a combination of many factors. Our weather includes:

• Temperature, from blistering heat to shivering cold.

• Cloud cover, from clear blue to dull and overcast skies.

• Wind speed and direction, from a light, warm breeze to a biting cold wind.

• Precipitation – the overall name for rain, hail, sleet, snow, frost and dew.

• Humidity, that is the amount of water vapour in the air. This varies from dry to very humid.

• Atmospheric conditions such as haze, mist, fog and smog.

Weather is caused by the Sun. The Sun's heat warms air and makes it move, creating winds. It warms water and makes ocean currents (see page 28). It also evaporates water into water vapour, which rises and forms clouds (see pages 30-31).

As water droplets and ice particles rise and fall and rub together inside a cloud, they produce an electrical charge. This leaps to another cloud or down to the surface as a gigantic spark of electricity – a lightning bolt.

FORECASTS

Modern weather forecasting uses thousands of weather stations all over the globe. They record wind, rain, sunshine and other conditions, and beam the results by satellite or telephone line to meteorology, or weather, centres. Weather ships and balloons also gather records.

In meteorology centres, computers process this mass of information, compare it with the usual weather patterns, and predict what will happen over the coming hours and days.

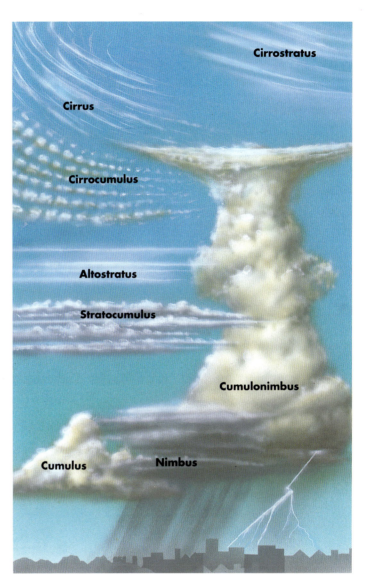

Different types of clouds form at different heights. The lower, darker clouds give rain. Towering cumulonimbus clouds produce hailstorms and thunderstorms. The highest cirrus and cirrostratus clouds are made up of floating ice crystals.

The energy of moving air – wind – can be used to spin angled blades. Windmills use wind power to grind grain and pump water. Modern wind farms generate electricity. They produce little noise and no air pollution. The wind generators shown here are in California, USA.

The symbols on this map show different aspects of the weather. The bare lines are isobars and they indicate air pressure. The closer they are, the stronger the winds. An area of high pressure usually means settled conditions and clear skies. A low pressure area brings cloud and rain.

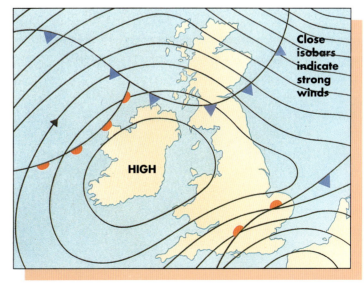

◈ TROPIC TO POLE

If you could walk from the Equator to the North Pole, you would notice gradual changes along the way. Lush tropical forests give way to open grasslands, and maybe a dry desert. You then reach mixed shrublands, and broadleaved woodlands. These are followed by conifer forests, then a cold treeless tundra, and finally the ice of the far north. These changing landscapes are produced by the varying climate right across the world.

Sun's rays

Temperature differences are due partly to the Earth's curved shape. At the Equator, some of the Sun's warmth goes through the atmosphere at right angles and falls on to a small surface area. Near the Pole, this same amount of warmth passes through more atmosphere, which absorbs some of it, and spreads the heat over a wider surface area.

CLIMATE

Weather is what happens in the atmosphere hour by hour and day by day. The weather conditions over much longer time periods, such as years and centuries, are called climate.

The climate varies due to temperature, which falls as you travel from Equator to Pole. It is also due to rainfall, which tends to be greater near the coasts and less in the middle of continents. Winds and ocean currents also have a great effect on climate.

Permanent ice and snow

Bare rocky scree

Alpine tundra

Alpine pasture

Treeline

Temperature falls with increasing height. This produces bands or zones on a tall mountain. As you climb up the mountain, you pass through zones similar to those you would see when travelling from Tropic to Pole.

Conifer trees

Broad-leaved forest on foothills

Tropical forest on lowlands

BIOMES

The climate in a region affects the kinds of plants which grow there. In turn, this affects the animals which can survive there. So the climate pattern produces broad regions around the world, called biomes or biogeographical zones.

TROPICS

Where it is warm and moist, life flourishes. The warmest region of the Earth is the Tropics, around the middle. The richest places for plants and animals are the tropical rainforests, where it is hot and wet nearly all year round.

In drier tropical places, trees give way to shrublands, then tropical grasslands. If it is very dry, this creates hot deserts where living things can hardly survive.

This map shows the main biogeographical zones with their characteristic plants and animals. Much of the world's natural vegetation, once forests and shrublands, has been removed and is now covered with crops and farm animals.

TEMPERATE LANDS

The regions between the Tropics and the Poles are called temperate lands. Here, it is quite cold in winter and fairly warm in summer, but the climate is not extreme.

In the wetter temperate areas, broad-leaved trees such as oak and beech form woodlands. In drier places there are temperate grasslands, like the prairies of North America and the steppes of Asia.

TOWARDS THE POLES

As the temperature falls nearer the polar regions, broad-leaved trees are replaced by needle-leaved trees such as pines, spruces and firs. These are suited to withstanding the long, cold, snowy winters. Summer is warm but brief.

Where it is colder still, trees cannot survive. The only vegetation is stunted bushes, small cushion-like plants, and mosses and lichens. This is the treeless tundra, which is covered by ice and snow for many months each year.

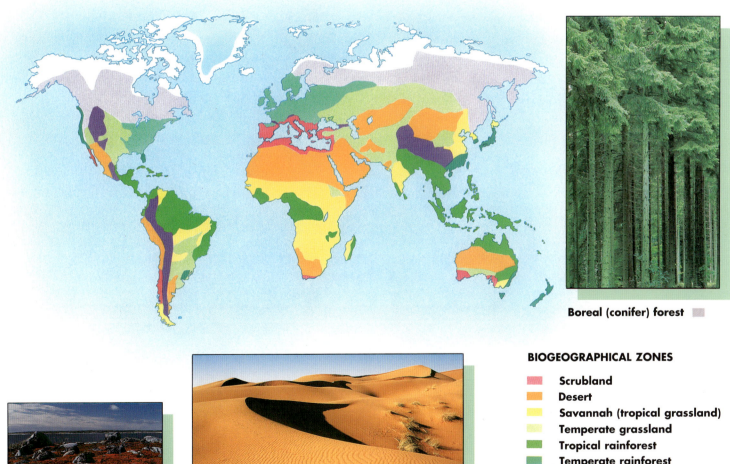

Desert 🟧

Tundra ▢

Boreal (conifer) forest ▢

BIOGEOGRAPHICAL ZONES

🟥 **Scrubland**
🟧 **Desert**
🟨 **Savannah (tropical grassland)**
🟩 **Temperate grassland**
🟩 **Tropical rainforest**
🟩 **Temperate rainforest**
🟩 **Temperate (broadleaved) forest**
⬜ **Boreal (conifer) forest**
🟪 **Mountain**
⬜ **Ice cap**
▢ **Tundra**

39

RUINING THE LANDSCAPE

Some of the richest wildlife on Earth lives in warm, wet tropical forests. The huge trees, vines and creepers, bushes and exotic flowers provide food and homes to vast numbers of animals. Native people may live in the forest too, taking only what they need and causing little damage.

NEW ARRIVALS

However, the forest's riches soon attract other people. Loggers make a road into the forest. They cut down trees and haul the trunks on to trucks. The logs are cut up in sawmills and sold as timber to people in distant lands.

Farmers arrive next. They drag out the tree stumps, and burn away any remaining plants in huge fires that darken the skies for days. Then they plant crops and spray them with chemicals to help them grow quickly. The crops are harvested and sold in distant countries.

MORE NEW ARRIVALS

Then the cattle ranchers come, bringing cows and other farm animals to graze on the newly-cleared land. The animals' meat is used to make steaks and hamburgers, for people in rich lands far away.

WORN-OUT SOIL

But the forest soil is thin. The crops take all the soil's nourishment and the animals soon graze the land bare. Few plants can grow there now. With no trees to shelter the land and no plant roots to hold the soil, heavy rains wash it into the river. The soil clogs up the river, and the river bursts its banks in a flood.

SAVING THE LANDSCAPE

People have realized what is happening just in time, so these disasters can be avoided in the future. The loggers can plant native trees to replace those that were destroyed. These will protect the soil. Only a few are cut down for timber each year and new ones are planted.

The farmers plant small fields of various crops which are suited to the soil and climate. They graze fewer cattle, and move the herd on regularly so that they do not wear out one area.

Some areas where the forest has grown back have been made into wildlife reserves. Tourists from well-off countries come to visit these parks to see their rare plants and animals.

THE POLLUTED EARTH

Ten thousand years ago, there were probably just five million people on Earth. Most lived a simple life as part of nature. Today, there are over five thousand million people and our way of life is damaging the Earth. We are using up the world's resources much faster than they can be replaced, and we risk upsetting our planet's natural balance.

The Sun's heat goes through the atmosphere, where some of it is absorbed. It reaches the Earth's surface, where more of it is absorbed. The rest is reflected back, and some of it is absorbed by greenhouse gases while the rest escapes into Space.

SUN

GLOBAL WARMING

Certain gases in the atmosphere help to trap and keep in the Sun's heat. They are called greenhouse gases. There has been a natural balance for millions of years. But now we are making more greenhouse gases. The main one is carbon dioxide, which comes from burning of any kind – forests, home fires, in petrol engines and so on. With more greenhouse gases, the Earth may get warmer. Ice caps will melt and the seas will rise, flooding vast areas of land. Global warming could be a terrible threat.

Reflected heat is absorbed by greenhouse gases

Heat is reflected from the oceans

Heat is reflected from the land

DAMAGING THE EARTH

People have been damaging and polluting the Earth for centuries, with their activities, leftovers and wastes. But today the damage is far greater, because there are so many of us, and because of the way we live. We drive cars, buy consumer goods and eat food grown on hi-tech farms and processed in factories. All this uses up vast amounts of raw materials and energy.

Many of the things we buy are made of metals. These come from rocks called ores that are dug from the ground. The resulting holes scar great areas of the landscape. Other items are made of plastic. This comes from oil which is obtained from deep wells. We are using vast amounts of oil, and it will eventually run out.

Fumes from power stations and vehicle exhausts contain chemicals which dissolve in the water droplets of clouds and fall as acid rain, harming trees and wildlife.

A computer map shows the 'ozone hole' - thinned ozone (white, pink and blue) over the South Pole and Antarctica. The thinning has worsened every year for 20 years, and there is also thinned ozone over northern regions.

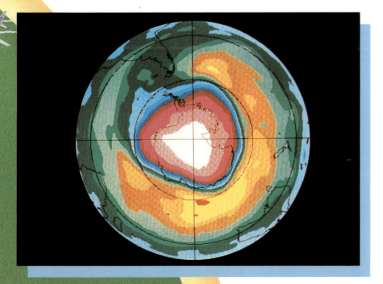

A mountain of old cars represents huge amounts of now-useless materials and energy. Great quantities of rock ores were mined for the metals. Heat and other energies were used to shape the cars' parts. Petrol and other polluting fuels powered the cars.

UNSEEN DANGERS

Some forms of pollution are obvious to our eyes, like piles of litter and rusting cars on a scrap heap. There are also many unseen pollutants. An example involves a gas in the atmosphere called ozone. There are only tiny amounts of ozone mixed in with normal air, mainly at a level between 15 and 30 kilometres high. This is called the ozone layer. The ozone filters out harmful rays from the Sun, called UV rays.

However, certain chemicals that are used in aerosol sprays and fridge coolants, and also to make packaging, destroy ozone. These chemicals are finding their way into the atmosphere, making the ozone layer thinner. The ozone layer above the polar regions is showing most signs of damage so far. The thinned areas are called 'ozone holes' and they let more UV light through to the Earth. UV light can cause sunburn, skin cancers and other health problems in people, and also diseases in animals.

TAKING ACTION

Many nations of the world have recognized the risks from ozone thinning. They have signed agreements to stop the use of ozone-destroying chemicals, and to find safer alternatives. But this will take many years.

There may also be other problems, as yet unseen and undiscovered, which will damage our Earth in the future.

LOOKING AFTER OUR EARTH

People are gradually becoming more aware of the problems facing the Earth. We know more about pollution, using up natural resources, and the dangers to wildlife and natural places. Knowing about these problems is the first step. The second step, solving them, will need much greater efforts. Yet everyone can help in some way, from governments and industries, to you and me. Here are some of the steps we can take.

SAVE ENERGY

We use energy in almost everything we do. Our homes, schools, factories, offices, engines, heaters and other machines, all use energy. Most of it comes from burning coal, oil, gas and other fossil fuels. At present rates, we will soon use these fuels up.

People are looking for renewable energy for tomorrow (see page 46). But you can help by saving energy today, in numerous ways. For example, cars use up fuel energy and create air pollution. You could help by avoiding using cars where you can. Walk or go by bicycle instead, both of which are healthier. Or use public transport. Try to share cars as much as possible to save on fuel energy.

This dustbin shows the breakdown of waste in a typical household. On average, at least half the contents of a bin could be recycled.

OUT SHOPPING

You may not like shopping for boring things, such as food and household items, but this is where you can have a great effect. Talk to your parents, or whoever does the shopping, about the purchases they make. Think about each product, and ask whether it is helping or harming the environment and the Earth.

For example, avoid wooden items that are made from tropical hardwoods, unless these are grown in a sustainable way, that is, when new trees are planted to replace those chopped down. Check household chemicals such as washing powders, detergents and bleaches. Are they environmentally friendly – that is, do they cause the minimum of damage to our surroundings? Do their containers rot away harmlessly, or can they be recycled? Try to avoid products that use a great deal of unnecessary packaging.

Cars clogging city streets are bad news all round. They waste fuel, pollute the air, create smog and dust, cause dangers for pedestrians, and waste their drivers' time.

AT HOME

You can cut down on the household fuel bills by switching off lights and electrical gadgets when they are not needed. This saves electricity, which saves energy at the local power station. You could check that your house, school and any other buildings are well-insulated to prevent heat escaping. Wasted heat is wasted energy.

Water is a precious resource. Making it clean is expensive. So, try thinking of ways to save water. You could take a shower instead of a bath. Or, if you do have a bath, maybe you could re-use your bathwater to water the garden or clean the car. Make sure that dripping taps get mended. And try to avoid using garden hoses for too long a time.

Recycling is becoming big business. Aluminium, iron, tin and other metals can be recovered from old cans, rather than digging up and processing new ores.

RECYCLING

When you thow away rubbish, it's a double-waste. Once because you no longer need it, and twice because it is a wasted opportunity to use it again. Recycling saves energy and raw materials. So, take bottles, cans, textiles, card and paper to suitable recycling banks. If there are none nearby, ask your local authority why not. And look for goods made from recycled materials in the shops.

You can recycle natural products, too. Build a compost heap to rot down leftover food and garden wastes so they are returned to the soil.

YOUR SURROUNDINGS

In your area, there might be a local group that you could join which works for the environment. Maybe you could help at a local nature reserve or wildlife park, or with a clean-up campaign such as saving a pond or wood. Or perhaps you could persuade your teachers to start a school project for the environment.

The area of truly wild places in the world is shrinking. As more people visit them, they disturb animals, pick plants, erode paths and leave litter. It is very important to follow the countryside code and protect nature. These people are rebuilding a hill path.

THE EARTH IN THE FUTURE

Scientists and conservationists have now started working together to study pollution, waste, the destruction of natural places, and disappearing resources. Their concern is how to save the Earth for people in the future.

One of the greatest problems of today is the increasing number of people, especially in over-populated towns and cities. And, looking to the future, the increase in world population shows no sign of slowing down.

WISHES AND WANTS

Most people would like to live in a 'green and pleasant land'. We want clean air, pure water, rich soils, and plenty of plants, animals, and unspoilt wilderness. Yet many people also want luxury homes, electrical gadgets, fast cars and flights to holidays in exotic places.

These two aims may seem opposed to each other. Cars and washing machines are made in factories, yet we do not want noisy, smoky factories just along the road. Cheap food is grown on huge farms, yet we do not want vast fields of boring crops or sheds packed with battery hens. Jet planes carry us on exciting holidays, yet they pollute the high atmosphere.

SHARING THE EARTH'S RESOURCES

There is a great gap in the way the Earth's resources are spread. The rich countries have trappings of luxury. In poor countries, thousands of people die daily from disease, and lack of good food and clean water.

A BALANCING ACT

The solutions to all these demands may come in time to save our Earth from further mass damage. They will probably also come from various sources.

Scientific research may help to clean up pollution and develop more efficient engines, less wasteful industrial processes, and cleaner, greener factories. Conservation workers may make us more aware of our surroundings, and how we can act to save resources and wildlife. Governments may begin to see that we need more co-operation in the world, and fairer shares of resources. People may change their ways and attitudes, too. In the future, we may value health and happiness more, as we enjoy the beauties and wonders of our home planet, Earth.

RENEWABLE ENERGY

There are many sources of energy besides fossil fuels. Some of these are renewable, which means that, as we use them carefully, they will be replaced naturally, for thousands of years to come.
Usually, the energy source is converted into our favourite form of power, electricity, which is fairly easy to transport along wires. But with each different source of energy, there is always some drawback.

SOLAR ENERGY
Capturing heat and light from the Sun.
Benefits: Free energy from the Sun, which will last for millions of years.
Drawbacks: Only obtainable in a few hot, sunny places. Needs more research for efficient conversion to electricity. Expensive to build.

WAVES AND TIDAL ENERGY
Barriers, tilting 'ducks' and similar devices harness the power of moving water.
Benefits: Free energy from waves and tides.
Drawbacks: Expensive to research and build suitable machinery. Causes changes in tides and currents that can then affect wildlife. Spoils the scenery.

THE RISE OF THE ECO-TOURIST

In many regions, activities such as logging and farming (see pages 40-41) earn money. But this is only for a few years. The land soon becomes barren and profits then disappear. Hunting rare wild animals also provides money. But, in time, the animals will be hunted to extinction.

Some countries are realizing that their natural landscapes and wildlife are very valuable. Tourists from richer countries pay large amounts of money to see rare animals and plants. This is called eco-tourism. It can earn money while hardly damaging the environment. But it must be carefully planned and controlled, or it could destroy the Earth's natural balance.

People can travel across the African grasslands silently by balloon, to watch the animals without disturbing them too much. But almost any type of tourism causes some problem, somewhere. The key is to minimize it.

WIND ENERGY
Modern windmills and wind farms harness the energy of moving air, caused by the Sun's warmth.
Benefits: Free energy from the wind.
Drawbacks: Available only in certain places. Spoils the scenery. Expensive to set up buildings and machinery. Does not product great amounts of electricity.

BIOMASS ENERGY
Burning plant matter, or rotting it down and then burning the gases it gives off.
Benefits: With good planning, it can be sustainable – it is really energy from the Sun, trapped by plants.
Drawbacks: Needs lots of space to grow the plants. Burning gives off greenhouse gases.

GEOTHERMAL ENERGY
Heat energy from deep in the Earth.
Benefits: Free energy from inside the Earth, which will last for millions of years.
Drawbacks: Available in only a few places. Sometimes unpredictable. Expensive to drill down and build suitable machinery.

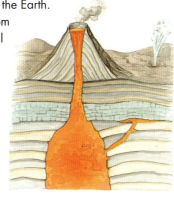

HYDROELECTRIC ENERGY
Dams and turbines trap the energy of water flowing downhill due to the Earth's gravity.
Benefits: Free energy. Can generate lots of electricity. Water is available for irrigating the land.
Drawbacks: Available only in certain places. Diverts rivers and spoils the scenery. Expensive to set up buildings and machinery.

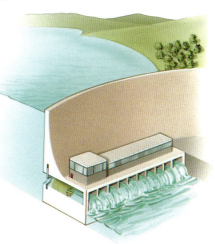

abyssal plain 27
acid rain 18, 32, 43
ammonoids 22
atmosphere 30, 34-35, 42, 43
atmospheric pressure 34, 35
aurorae 35

basalt 13
biogeographical zones 39
boreholes 6, 23
breccias 21

caves 32-33
climate 38-39
clouds 30, 31, 36, 37
coal 23, 24, 44
coastal erosion 28-29
conglomerates 21
continental crust 7, 27
continental drift 8-9
continental shelves 26, 27
core 6, 7
crust 6, 7, 8, 9

deep-sea vents 27
deserts 39
diamonds 12, 24
dinosaurs 20, 22
discontinuities 6

earthquakes 9, 10-11
eclipse 5
eco-tourism 47
energy conservation 44-45
energy sources 46-47
environmentally friendly products 44
Equator 6, 38
erosion 18, 19, 20
    caves 32-33
    coasts 28-29
evaporation 31
extinct volcanoes 16-17

farming 40-41, 47
faults 9, 11
fishing 25
flint 21
fold mountains 14, 15
fossils 22-23
fuels 25, 44
    fossil 23, 44, 46

gas (fuel) 23, 25, 43, 44
gases 34
greenhouse 42, 47
geothermal energy 47
geysers 30
glaciers 19, 30

global warming 42
gold 24
gorge 19
granite 12, 13
gravity 29, 34, 47

humidity 36
hydroelectric energy 47

ice 18, 19, 30, 31
igneous rock 12, 13, 14, 22
isobars 37

lakes 30, 31
lightning 36
limestone 21, 32-33
lithospheric plates 8-9, 10, 14, 26, 27
logging 40, 47

magma 12, 13, 30
    volcanoes 16-17, 26, 27
magnetic poles 7
mantle 6, 7, 9, 14, 26
marble 15
mesosphere 34-35
metal ores 24, 43
metamorphic rocks 13, 14-15, 22
meteorites 34
meteorology centres 37
mid-oceanic ridge 8, 9, 27
minerals 12, 24-25, 33
mining 24
Moon 4, 5, 29
moraine 19
mountains 15
    climate zones 38
    formation 8, 14

ocean currents 28, 36, 38
oceanic crust 7, 27
ocean trenches 26, 27
oil 23, 25, 43, 44
oil wells 6, 23, 25
orbit 5
oxygen 34, 35
ozone layer 43

Pangaea 8
planets 4, 5
plants 19, 23, 30
plates 8-9, 10, 11, 14, 27
poles 6, 7, 38
pollution 42-43, 44-45, 46
population increase 46
pothole 33
power stations 29, 43
precipitation 36
prehistoric life 22

rain 18, 30, 31
rainfall 38
recycling 45
resources 24-25, 42
Richter scale 10
rivers 30, 31
rock formation 12-13, 14

sandstone 20, 21
sea defences 29
seas 25, 30
seasons 5, 36
sedimentary rock 12, 13, 20-21, 22
seismic waves 10, 25
shales 21
silica 12
slate 15
snow 19, 30, 36, 39
soil erosion 41
solar energy 46
Solar System 5
sonar 25, 26, 27
spits 28
stacks 28
stalactites 33
stalagmites 33
stratosphere 34-35
subduction zones 26
Sun 4, 5
    erosion 18
    tides 29
    water cycle 31
    weather 28, 36, 38

temperate lands 39
temperature 18, 36, 38
thermosphere 35
tides 29
    energy 29, 46
tropical rainforests 39, 40
troposphere 34-35
tsunamis 11
tundra 39

valleys 19
volcanoes 12-13, 14, 16-17, 26

waste 44, 46
water 30-31, 45
    erosion 18, 19
    vapour 31, 36
waves 28, 46
    tidal 11
weather 36-37, 38
weathering 18, 20
windmills 37, 47
winds 28, 36, 38
    erosion 18